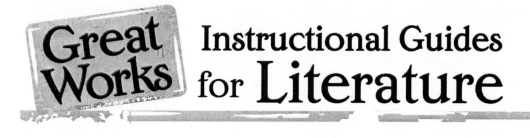

Great Works Instructional Guides for Literature

Thunder Boy Jr.

A guide for the book by Sherman Alexie
Great Works Author: Tom Schiele

SHELL EDUCATION

Publishing Credits

Corinne Burton, M.A.Ed., *President*; Conni Medina, M.A.Ed., *Managing Editor*; Emily R. Smith, M.A.Ed., *Content Director*; Lee Aucoin, *Senior Graphic Designer*; Stephanie Bernard, *Assistant Editor*; Don Tran, *Graphic Designer*

Image Credits

Cover design & illustration Lee Aucoin; background image iStock

Standards

© 2007 Teachers of English to Speakers of Other Languages, Inc. (TESOL)
© 2007 Board of Regents of the University of Wisconsin System. World-Class Instructional Design and Assessment (WIDA)
© Copyright 2010. National Governors Association Center for Best Practices and Council of Chief State School Officers. All rights reserved.
© Copyright 2007–2015. Texas Education Association (TEA). All rights reserved.

Shell Education

A division of Teacher Created Materials
5301 Oceanus Drive
Huntington Beach, CA 92649-1030

ISBN 978-1-4258-1720-6

https://www.tcmpub.com/shell-education
© 2017 Shell Educational Publishing, Inc.

Table of contents

How to Use This Literature Guide

Today's standards demand rigor and relevance in the reading of complex texts. The units in this series guide teachers in a rich and deep exploration of worthwhile works of literature for classroom study. The most rigorous instruction can also be interesting and engaging!

Many current strategies for effective literacy instruction have been incorporated into these instructional guides for literature. Throughout the units, text-dependent questions are used to determine comprehension of the book as well as student interpretation of the vocabulary words. The books chosen for the series are complex and are exemplars of carefully crafted works of literature. Close reading is used throughout the units to guide students toward revisiting the text and using textual evidence to respond to prompts orally and in writing. Students must analyze the story elements in multiple assignments for each section of the book. All of these strategies work together to rigorously guide students through their study of literature.

The next few pages describe how to use this guide for a purposeful and meaningful literature study. Each section of this guide is set up in the same way to make it easier for you to implement the instruction in your classroom.

Theme Thoughts

The great works of literature used throughout this series have important themes that have been relevant to people for many years. Many of the themes will be discussed during the various sections of this instructional guide. However, it would also benefit students to have independent time to think about the key themes of the book.

Before students begin reading, have them complete the *Pre-Reading Theme Thoughts* (page 13). This graphic organizer will allow students to think about the themes outside the context of the story. They'll have the opportunity to evaluate statements based on important themes and defend their opinions. Be sure to keep students' papers for comparison to the *Post-Reading Theme Thoughts* (page 59). This graphic organizer is similar to the pre-reading activity. However, this time, students will be answering the questions from the point of view of one of the characters in the book. They have to think about how the character would feel about each statement and defend their thoughts. To conclude the activity, have students compare what they thought about the themes before they read the book to what the characters discovered during the story.

How to Use This Literature Guide (cont.)

Vocabulary

Each teacher reference vocabulary overview page has definitions and sentences about how key vocabulary words are used in the section. These words should be introduced and discussed with students. Students will use these words in different activities throughout the book.

On some of the vocabulary student pages, students are asked to answer text-related questions about vocabulary words from the sections. The following question stems will help you create your own vocabulary questions if you'd like to extend the discussion.

- How does this word describe _____'s character?
- How does this word connect to the problem in this story?
- How does this word help you understand the setting?
- Tell me how this word connects to the main idea of this story.
- What visual pictures does this word bring to your mind?
- Why do you think the author used this word?

At times, you may find that more work with the words will help students understand their meanings and importance. These quick vocabulary activities are a good way to further study the words.

- Students can play vocabulary concentration. Make one set of cards that has the words on them and another set with the definitions. Then, have students lay them out on the table and play concentration. The goal of the game is to match vocabulary words with their definitions. For early readers or English language learners, the two sets of cards could be the words and pictures of the words.

- Students can create word journal entries about the words. Students choose words they think are important and then describe why they think each word is important within the book. Early readers or English language learners could instead draw pictures about the words in a journal.

- Students can create puppets and use them to act out the vocabulary words from the stories. Students may also enjoy telling their own character-driven stories using vocabulary words from the original stories.

How to Use This Literature Guide (cont.)

Analyzing the Literature

After you have read each section with students, hold a small-group or whole-class discussion. Provided on the teacher reference page for each section are leveled questions. The questions are written at two levels of complexity to allow you to decide which questions best meet the needs of your students. The Level 1 questions are typically less abstract than the Level 2 questions. These questions are focused on the various story elements, such as character, setting, and plot. Be sure to add further questions as your students discuss what they've read. For each question, a few key points are provided for your reference as you discuss the book with students.

Reader Response

In today's classrooms, there are often great readers who are below average writers. So much time and energy is spent in classrooms getting students to read on grade level that little time is left to focus on writing skills. To help teachers include more writing in their daily literacy instruction, each section of this guide has a literature-based reader response prompt. Each of the three genres of writing is used in the reader responses within this guide: narrative, informative/explanatory, and opinion. Before students write, you may want to allow them time to draw pictures related to the topic. Book-themed writing paper is provided on page 69 if your students need more space to write.

Guided Close Reading

Within each section of this guide, it is suggested that you closely reread a portion of the text with your students. The sections to be reread are described by location within the story since there are no page numbers in these books. After rereading the section, there are a few text-dependent questions to be answered by students.

Working space has been provided to help students prepare for the group discussion. They should record their thoughts and ideas on the activity page and refer to it during your discussion. Rather than just taking notes, you may want to require students to write complete responses to the questions before discussing them with you.

Encourage students to read one question at a time and then go back to the text and discover the answer. Work with students to ensure that they use the text to determine their answers rather than making unsupported inferences. Suggested answers are provided in the answer key.

How to Use This Literature Guide (cont.)

Guided Close Reading (cont.)

The generic open-ended stems below can be used to write your own text-dependent questions if you would like to give students more practice.

- What words in the story support . . . ?
- What text helps you understand . . . ?
- Use the book to tell why _____ happens.
- Based on the events in the story, . . . ?
- Show me the part in the text that supports . . . .
- Use the text to tell why . . . .

Making Connections

The activities in this section help students make cross-curricular connections to mathematics, science, social studies, fine arts, or other curricular areas. These activities require higher-order thinking skills from students but also allow for creative thinking.

Language Learning

A special section has been set aside to connect the literature to language conventions. Through these activities, students will have opportunities to practice the conventions of standard English grammar, usage, capitalization, and punctuation.

Story Elements

It is important to spend time discussing what the common story elements are in literature. Understanding the characters, setting, plot, and theme can increase students' comprehension and appreciation of the story. If teachers begin discussing these elements in early childhood, students will more likely internalize the concepts and look for the elements in their independent reading. Another very important reason for focusing on the story elements is that students will be better writers if they think about how the stories they read are constructed.

In the story elements activities, students are asked to create work related to the characters, setting, or plot. Consider having students complete only one of these activities. If you give students a choice on this assignment, each student can decide to complete the activity that most appeals to him or her. Different intelligences are used so that the activities are diverse and interesting to all students.

How to Use This Literature Guide (cont.)

Culminating Activity

At the end of this instructional guide is a creative culminating activity that allows students the opportunity to share what they've learned from reading the book. This activity is open ended so that students can push themselves to create their own great works within your language arts classroom.

Comprehension Assessment

The questions in this section require students to think about the book they've read as well as the words that were used in the book. Some questions are tied to quotations from the book to engage students and require them to think about the text as they answer the questions.

Response to Literature

Finally, students are asked to respond to the literature by drawing pictures and writing about the characters and story. A suggested rubric is provided for teacher reference.

Correlation to the Standards

Shell Education is committed to producing educational materials that are research and standards based. As part of this effort, we have correlated all of our products to the academic standards of all 50 states, the District of Columbia, the Department of Defense Dependents Schools, and all Canadian provinces.

Purpose and Intent of Standards

The Every Student Succeeds Act (ESSA) mandates that all states adopt challenging academic standards that help students meet the goal of college and career readiness. While many states already adopted academic standards prior to ESSA, the act continues to hold states accountable for detailed and comprehensive standards. Standards are statements that describe the criteria necessary for students to meet specific academic goals. They define the knowledge, skills, and content students should acquire at each level. State standards are used in the development of our products, so educators can be assured they meet state academic requirements.

How to Find Standards Correlations

To print a customized correlation report of this product for your state, visit our website at **www.teachercreated materials.com/administrators/correlations/** and follow the online directions. If you require assistance in printing correlation reports, please contact our Customer Service Department at 1-877-777-3450.

correlation to the Standards (cont.)

Standards correlation chart

The lessons in this book were written to support today's college and career readiness standards. The following chart indicates which lessons address each standard.

College and Career Readiness Standard	Section
Read closely to determine what the text says explicitly and to make logical inferences from it; cite specific textual evidence when writing or speaking to support conclusions drawn from the text.	Guided Close Reading Sections 1–5; Analyzing the Literature Sections 1–5
Determine central ideas or themes of a text and analyze their development; summarize the key supporting details and ideas.	Analyzing the Literature Sections 1–5
Analyze how and why individuals, events, or ideas develop and interact over the course of a text.	Guided Close Reading Sections 1–5; Analyzing the Literature Sections 1–5; Story Elements Sections 1–5
Interpret words and phrases as they are used in a text, including determining technical, connotative, and figurative meanings, and analyze how specific word choices shape meaning or tone.	Vocabulary Sections 1–5
Analyze the structure of texts, including how specific sentences, paragraphs, and larger portions of the text (e.g., a section, chapter, scene, or stanza) relate to each other and the whole.	Guided Close Reading Sections 1–5; Story Elements Sections 1, 3, 5
Read and comprehend complex literary and informational texts independently and proficiently.	Entire Unit
Write arguments to support claims in an analysis of substantive topics or texts using valid reasoning and relevant and sufficient evidence.	Reader Response Sections 1, 4
Write informative/explanatory texts to examine and convey complex ideas and information clearly and accurately through the effective selection, organization, and analysis of content.	Reader Response Section 3; Culminating Activity
Write narratives to develop real or imagined experiences or events using effective technique, well-chosen details and well-structured event sequences.	Reader Response Sections 2, 5
Conduct short as well as more sustained research projects based on focused questions, demonstrating understanding of the subject under investigation.	Making Connections Sections 2, 5
Present information, findings, and supporting evidence such that listeners can follow the line of reasoning and the organization, development, and style are appropriate to task, purpose, and audience.	Culminating Activity

correlation to the standards (cont.)

standards correlation chart (cont.)

College and Career Readiness Standard	Section
Demonstrate command of the conventions of standard English grammar and usage when writing or speaking.	Language Learning Sections 1–5; Reader Response Sections 1–5; Culminating Activity
Demonstrate command of the conventions of standard English capitalization, punctuation, and spelling when writing.	Reader Response Sections 1–5; Culminating Activity
Determine or clarify the meaning of unknown and multiple-meaning words and phrases by using context clues, analyzing meaningful word parts, and consulting general and specialized reference materials, as appropriate.	Vocabulary Sections 1–5
Demonstrate understanding of figurative language, word relationships, and nuances in word meanings.	Language Learning Sections 3–5

TESOL and WIDA Standards

The lessons in this book promote English language development for English language learners. The following TESOL and WIDA English Language Development Standards are addressed through the activities in this book:

- **Standard 1:** English language learners communicate for social and instructional purposes within the school setting.

- **Standard 2:** English language learners communicate information, ideas and concepts necessary for academic success in the content area of language arts.

About the Author—Sherman Alexie

Sherman Alexie is a poet, short story writer, novelist, and performer. A Spokane/Coeur d'Alene Indian, he grew up on the Spokane Indian Reservation in Wellpinit, Washington.

Alexie was born with hydrocephalus, a condition in which there is an abnormally large amount of cerebral fluid in the cranial cavity. He had to have brain surgery when he was six months old. The surgery was successful, but as a child, his head was abnormally large. He was nicknamed "The Globe," and he was constantly teased by other kids. While he was excluded from many activities, Alexie became an avid reader, consuming everything available, including auto repair manuals.

As an adolescent, Alexie decided to leave the reservation, traveling 22 miles (35 km) to attend Rearden High School, where he was the only American Indian student. He continued to excel academically and became a star basketball player. He entered college with the intention of becoming a doctor. Then, he switched to law before finally being introduced to creative writing.

Alexie has published 25 books. Perhaps his best-known, *The Lone Ranger and Tonto Fistfight in Heaven*, is a collection of stories. His books for young readers include a young adult novel, *The Absolutely True Diary of a Part-Time Indian,* and *Thunder Boy Jr.,* which is his first picture book.

Alexie is the winner of the PEN/Faulkner Award for Fiction, the PEN/Malamud Award for Short Fiction, the PEN/Hemingway Citation for Best First Fiction, and the National Book Award for Young People's Literature. He also wrote and co-produced the 1998 movie *Smoke Signals.* The film went on to win the Audience Award and Filmmakers Trophy at the 1998 Sundance Film Festival®.

Possible Texts for Text Comparisons

A good comparison text to *Thunder Boy Jr.* is Kevin Henkes's classic picture book, *Chrysanthemum.* This story is similar to *Thunder Boy Jr.* in its focus on how a name affects young people.

Cross-Curricular Connection

Thunder Boy Jr. can be incorporated into a primary social studies unit on the self or a unit on American Indians.

Book Summary of *Thunder Boy Jr.*

Thunder Boy Jr. is named after his father, who is known as Big Thunder. This leaves Thunder Boy Jr. with the nickname Little Thunder. While he loves and respects his father, Thunder Boy Jr. tells the reader that he "hates his name." Thunder Boy Jr. tries on different monikers, all the while searching through his accomplishments, his likes and dislikes, and his hopes and dreams to find a name telling of who he is and what he has done. At last, Big Thunder recognizes his son's struggle and concludes: "I think it's time I gave you a new name. A name of your own." Thunder Boy Jr. is thrilled with his new name—Lightning—and together, father and son stride off over the clouds.

How to Read the Book

Thunder Boy Jr. is a picture book and doesn't have chapters. For the purposes of teaching this book with young readers, this guide has been divided into five sections. Each section of this instructional guide contains lessons and activities to help students gain an understanding of the story.

- **Section 1: Meet Thunder Boy Jr.**—In this section, readers are introduced to the protagonist, Thunder Boy Smith, and learn that he is named after his father. Readers also learn a secret—Thunder Boy Jr. hates his name.

- **Section 2: I Want a New Name**—This section focuses on the various activities Thunder Boy Jr. has done and the traits that he has. He uses these as inspiration as he brainstorms a new name for himself.

- **Section 3: Thunder Boy and Lightning**—In this section, Thunder Boy Jr.'s goal is achieved! Thunder Boy Jr. is given a new name—a name of his very own—by his father.

- **Section 4: Illustrations**—This section allows readers to focus on the lovely, colorful illustrations by Yuyi Morales and to think critically about what the illustrations add to the story.

- **Section 5: Whole Book**—This section looks at the whole book and focuses on the big picture.

Possible Texts for Text Sets

- Bruchac, Joseph and James. 2003. *How Chipmunk Got His Stripes.* New York: Puffin.
- Goble, Paul. 1991. *Star Boy.* New York: Aladdin.
- McDermott, Gerald. 2001. *Raven: A Trickster Tale from the Pacific Northwest.* Orlando: Voyager Books.
- Morales, Yuyi. 2015. *Nino Wrestles the World.* New York: Square Fish.
- Tonatiuh, Duncan. 2013. *Pancho Rabbit and the Coyote: A Migrant's Tale.* New York: Abrams.

Pre-Reading Theme Thoughts

Directions: Draw a picture of a happy face or a sad face. Your face should show how you feel about each statement. Then, use words to say what you think about each statement.

Statement	How Do You Feel? ☺ ☹	Why Do You Feel This Way?
Names are important.		
I like my name.		
I want a different name.		
I have many name ideas.		

Vocabulary Overview

Key words and phrases from this section are provided below with definitions and sentences about how the words are used in the story. Introduce and discuss these important vocabulary words with students. If you think these words or other words in the story warrant more time devoted to them, there are suggestions in the introduction for other vocabulary activities (page 5).

Word or Phrase	Definition	Sentence about Text
thunder	sound caused by lightning	**Thunder** is an unusual name for a boy.
real	not fake	Thunder Boy is his **real** name.
named after	given the same name as someone	Thunder Boy Jr. is **named after** his father.
nickname	another name	Big Thunder is a **nickname** that fills the sky.
normal	ordinary	Thunder Boy is not a **normal** name.
secret	something that is hidden away	Thunder Boy Jr. has a **secret**.
whisper	to speak very softly	Thunder Boy **whispers** a secret to the reader.
awesome	cool	Thunder Boy Jr. thinks his dad is **awesome**.

Name _____

Vocabulary Activity

Directions: Write the word from the story that best matches each clue.

Words from the Story

thunder	real	awesome	whisper	secret

1. This is when something is really cool.

   _____

   _____

2. This is the opposite of fake.

   _____

   _____

3. This is something you don't tell anyone.

   _____

   _____

4. First you see lightning, and then you hear this sound.

   _____

   _____

5. This is when you talk very quietly.

   _____

   _____

Teacher Plans

Analyzing the Literature

Provided below are discussion questions you can use in small groups, with the whole class, or for written assignments. Each question is written at two levels so that you can choose the right question for each group of students. For each question, a few key points are provided for your reference as you discuss the book with students.

Story Element	Level 1	Level 2	Key Discussion Points
Plot	Who is telling the story? How do you know?	Why is it important to have Thunder Boy Jr. tell the story?	Thunder Boy Jr. is telling the story. This is important because it lets him tell the reader his feelings about his name.
Character	How does Thunder Boy Jr. feel about his name?	How can you tell that Thunder Boy Jr. doesn't like his name?	Thunder Boy Jr. hates his name. You can tell because he keeps saying that Thunder Boy is not a normal name. He also screams, "I HATE MY NAME!"
Plot	What is Thunder Boy Jr.'s secret?	Why does Thunder Boy Jr. whisper his secret to the reader?	Thunder Boy Jr. hates his name. He whispers to the reader because he doesn't want his family to know his secret.
Setting	What is the setting of the book?	How do the illustrations help tell about the setting of the book?	The setting is not directly stated; however, it can be interpreted that the story takes place in Thunder Boy Jr.'s home or outside his home. The illustrations tell about the setting because they show where things are happening.

Reader Response

Think

In *Thunder Boy Jr.*, the main character is named after his father. Thunder Boy Jr. doesn't like his name. He wants to choose his own name.

Opinion Writing Prompt

Do you think people should choose their own names? Why or why not? Give reasons for your opinion.

_____

_____

_____

_____

_____

_____

_____

_____

_____

_____

_____

_____

_____

Guided Close Reading

Closely reread the first pages of the book. Start at the beginning. Stop with, "Thunder Boy is not a normal name."

Directions: Think about these questions. In the space below, write ideas or draw pictures as you think. Be ready to share your answers.

❶ Where is Thunder Boy Jr. on the first page of the book? What is he doing? Turn the page. What is he doing now?

❷ What do you notice about the family members?

❸ How does Thunder Boy Jr. feel about the name he was almost given? How can you tell?

Making connections—Make Thunder

Thunder is a sound made by lightning. When lightning strikes, it gives off energy. This heats the air around it. The hot air expands. It moves in a wave. The wave of air makes a loud sound.

Directions: Follow these directions to make your own thunder.

Materials

- brown paper bag

Instructions

1. Blow into the brown paper bag. Fill it up with air.

2. Twist the open end to close it.

3. Hit the bottom of the bag with your hand.

   - When you hit the bag, you make pressure in the bag. The pressure breaks the bag. The air inside rushes out. This pushes the air outside away from the bag. The air moves in a wave. When the wave of air reaches your ear, you hear a sound: thunder!

1. How would you describe the sound of thunder?

_____

- - - - - - - - - - - - - - - - - - -

_____

_____

- - - - - - - - - - - - - - - - - - -

Name _____

Language Learning—Verbs

Directions: Circle verbs in the sentences about the story. The first one has been done for you.

Language Hint!

Verbs are words that show action.

1. People (call) him Big Thunder.

2. His dad gave his name to him at birth.

3. A storm fills the sky.

4. Thunder Boy Jr. tells a secret.

5. He whispers the secret.

6. Thunder Boy Jr. calls his dad awesome.

Story Elements—character

Directions: Thunder Boy Jr. shows different emotions.
Draw pictures of two different emotions he feels. Then,
write a sentence to describe each picture.

Story Elements—Plot

Directions: Cut apart the cards below. Glue them on another sheet of paper in the order of the story.

Thunder Boy Jr. tells the reader a secret.	Thunder Boy Jr. tells the names of his mother and sister.
Readers learn how Thunder Boy Jr. feels about his dad.	Readers learn that Thunder Boy Jr. is named after his dad.
Thunder Boy Jr. tells readers that his name is not normal.	Readers learn Thunder Boy Jr. is his real name.

Vocabulary Overview

Key words and phrases from this section are provided below with definitions and sentences about how the words are used in the story. Introduce and discuss these important vocabulary words with students. If you think these words or other words in the story warrant more time devoted to them, there are suggestions in the introduction for other vocabulary activities (page 5).

Word or Phrase	Definition	Sentence about Text
celebrates	honors	Thunder Boy Jr. wants a name that **celebrates** what he has done.
orca	a kind of whale; also called a killer whale	Thunder Boy Jr. touches the nose of an **orca**.
climbed	traveled upwards	Thunder Boy Jr. once **climbed** a mountain.
gravity	force that pulls an object to the ground/earth	A new name for Thunder Boy Jr. could be **Gravity**'s Best Friend.
dreamed	imagined	Thunder Boy Jr. **dreams** the sun and moon are his parents.
garage sale	sales held in the seller's garage	Thunder Boy Jr. likes to go to **garage sales** with his mom.
powwow	American Indian celebration	Thunder Boy Jr. loves **powwow** dancing.
wonder	a feeling of awe	Full of **Wonder** might be a good name for Thunder Boy Jr.

Name _____

Vocabulary Activity

Directions: Practice your writing skills. Write at least two sentences using words from the story.

Words from the Story

dreamed	celebrates	orca	climbed
gravity	garage sale	powwow	wonder

_____

- -

_____

- -

_____

- -

_____

- -

_____

- -

_____

Directions: Answer this question.

1. What makes Thunder Boy Jr. full of **wonder**?

_____

- -

_____

Analyzing the Literature

Provided below are discussion questions you can use in small groups, with the whole class, or for written assignments. Each question is written at two levels so that you can choose the right question for each group of students. For each question, a few key points are provided for your reference as you discuss the book with students.

Story Element	Level 1	Level 2	Key Discussion Points
Character	How can you tell that Thunder Boy Jr. is close to his family?	Thunder Boy Jr.'s family shows up in each of his name ideas. What does this say about what family means to him?	Thunder Boy Jr.'s family shows up in each name idea because family is important to him. He wants a name that celebrates who he is, and his family is a part of who he is.
Character	Is Thunder Boy Jr. adventurous? How do you know?	How does the illustrator show Thunder Boy Jr.'s sense of adventure?	The illustrations show Thunder Boy Jr. touching the nose of a giant orca, on top of a mountain, and riding his bike through the mud while standing on the seat.
Plot	What is Thunder Boy Jr.'s dream?	Why does Thunder Boy Jr. suggest Full of Wonder as a new name?	Thunder Boy Jr. dreams of traveling all over the world. He suggests Full of Wonder because he wants to see and explore the world.
Setting	What are some of the settings you see?	Why does the setting change for each name Thunder Boy Jr. thinks of?	The settings include a mountain, in puddles of mud, an area or room with toys, and a powwow. The setting changes with each name to show Thunder Boy Jr. doing all the things he likes to do.

Name _____

Reader Response

Think

In *Thunder Boy Jr.*, the main character is trying to come up with a new name for himself. Think about how to choose a name.

Narrative Writing Prompt

Imagine you have a new pet. Write a story that tells how you would give it a name. Make sure to give reasons why it would be a good name for that pet.

_____

- -

_____

- -

_____

- -

_____

- -

_____

- -

_____

Guided Close Reading

Closely reread the pages where Thunder Boy Jr. thinks of new names. Start with, "I once dreamed." Stop with, "Drums, Drums, and More Drums."

Directions: Think about these questions. In the space below, write ideas or draw pictures as you think. Be ready to share your answers.

❶ What are the names Thunder Boy Jr. thinks of? Which is your favorite?

❷ Thunder Boy Jr. likes to go to garage sales. Whom does he go with? How do you think they get there?

❸ Who are the drummers for the grass dance? Where have you seen them before?

Name _____

Making connections—Orcas

Directions: Thunder Boy Jr. touches the nose of a wild orca. Orcas are whales. Do some research about orcas. Complete this chart.

Orcas	
Nickname	
Habitat	
Size	
Color	
Food	
Number of teeth	
Unusual fact	

Language Learning—Nouns

Directions: Look at the page that says, "Old toys are awesome!" List five nouns you see. Then, write a sentence using two of the nouns you listed.

Language Hint!

A noun is a person, place, thing, or idea.

_____

1. _____

2. _____

3. _____

4. _____

5. _____

My sentence: _____

Name _____

Story Elements—Character

Directions: Thunder Boy Jr. has different traits. Read the activities he has done. Then, match them with the trait that best describes Thunder Boy Jr.

adventurous	He touches an orca.
athletic	He climbs a mountain.
brave	He slides through mud.
playful	He rides a bike when he is three years old.

Story Elements—Setting

Directions: In *Thunder Boy Jr.,* there is a different setting for each possible name. For example, the setting for the name Mud in His Ears shows characters playing in the mud. Pick a name for Thunder Boy Jr. Then, draw a setting for the name.

Teacher Plans

Vocabulary Overview

Key words and phrases from this section are provided below with definitions and sentences about how the words are used in the story. Introduce and discuss these important vocabulary words with students. If you think these words or other words in the story warrant more time devoted to them, there are suggestions in the introduction for other vocabulary activities (page 5).

Word or Phrase	Definition	Sentence about Text
exactly	the same	Thunder Boy Jr. doesn't want to be **exactly** like his dad.
mostly	mainly; almost all	Thunder Boy Jr. wants to be **mostly** himself.
read my mind	knew what someone was thinking	Thunder Boy Jr. is happy his dad **read his mind**.
read my heart	knew what someone was feeling	Thunder Boy Jr.'s dad **read his heart**.
light up	brighten	Thunder Boy and Lightning **light up** the sky.
bright	very clear; filled with light; full of promise	The love between Thunder Boy and Lightning is **bright**.
loud	noisy	Together, Thunder Boy and Lightning are bright and **loud**.

Vocabulary Activity

Directions: Review the words and definitions. Then, answer the questions.

1. **mostly**—mainly; almost all

   Do you think you are **mostly** yourself? Why or why not?

   _____

   - - - - - - - - - - - - - - - - -

   _____

   - - - - - - - - - - - - - - - - -

   _____

2. **read my mind**—knew what someone was thinking

   Has anyone ever **read your mind**? What did he or she say?

   _____

   - - - - - - - - - - - - - - - - -

   _____

   - - - - - - - - - - - - - - - - -

   _____

3. **loud**—noisy

   When is it okay to speak in **loud** voices?

   _____

   - - - - - - - - - - - - - - - - -

   _____

   - - - - - - - - - - - - - - - - -

   _____

Teacher Plans

Analyzing the Literature

Provided below are discussion questions you can use in small groups, with the whole class, or for written assignments. Each question is written at two levels so that you can choose the right question for each group of students. For each question, a few key points are provided for your reference as you discuss the book with students.

Story Element	Level 1	Level 2	Key Discussion Points
Character	What does Thunder Boy Jr. say about his dad?	Tell about the relationship between Thunder Boy Jr. and his dad. Use examples to help you.	Thunder Boy Jr. says he loves his dad but he doesn't want to be exactly like him. Thunder Boy Jr. and his dad love each other. Thunder Boy understands his son. You can tell because Thunder Boy Jr. proclaims, "My dad read my mind! My dad read my heart!"
Plot	Look at the pages where Thunder Boy Jr. says he doesn't want to be exactly like his dad. What is happening?	What reasons does Thunder Boy Jr. give for not wanting the name he was given?	Thunder Boy Jr. is telling why he doesn't want to have his name. He says he doesn't want to be small. He also doesn't want to be exactly like his dad but instead wants to be mostly himself.
Plot	What changes after Thunder Boy Jr. is given a new name?	How can you tell Thunder Boy Jr. is happy to hear his dad say, "I think it's time I gave you a new name"?	At first, Thunder Boy Jr. is sad and upset. Then, he is smiling when he finds out that his dad wants to give him a new name—a name of his own.
Setting	How does the setting change?	What does the setting at the end of the book say about the characters?	The setting changes from a bright day to a stormy, gray day. This shows that father and son are strong and powerful when they are themselves but working together.

Reader Response

Think

People get their names in different ways. In *Thunder Boy Jr.*, readers learn how Thunder Boy Jr. got his name and how he gets a new one. Think about how you got your name.

Explanatory/Expository Writing Prompt

Write about how you got your name. Tell who gave it to you. Tell why they decided it was the perfect name for you.

_____

_____

_____

_____

_____

_____

_____

_____

_____

_____

Name _____

Guided close Reading

Closely reread the pages where Thunder Boy Jr. tells why he wants a new name. Start with, "I do not want the name ...." Stop with, "What do I say?"

Directions: Think about these questions. In the space below, write ideas or draw pictures as you think. Be ready to share your answers.

❶ Who says "Little Thunder"? How do you know?

❷ How can you tell Thunder Boy Jr. feels upset?

❸ Why does Thunder Boy Jr. make sure to say that he loves his dad?

Making connections—Weather

Directions: Think about the weather when there is thunder and lightning. Think about the weather when it is sunny. Fill in the chart below with words and pictures to compare the two types of weather. Then, answer the question.

Sunny	Thunder and Lightning

1. Which type of weather do you like more? Why?

_____

_____

_____

_____

Language Learning—Adjectives

Directions: Some adjectives from the story are listed in the chart. Find and list the nouns they describe.

Language Hint!

Adjectives are describing words.

Adjective	Noun	Adjective + Noun
Little	Thunder	Little Thunder
amazing		
bright		
loud		

Directions: Write a new sentence using two of the adjectives from the story.

_____

_____

_____

_____

_____

Story Elements—Character

Directions: Thunder Boy Jr.'s dad gives him a new name—Lightning. Imagine you are Lightning. Write your dad a letter telling him why you love your new name.

_____
– – – – – – – – – – – –
_____
_____
– –
_____
– –
_____
_____
– –
_____
– –
_____
                          _____
                          – – – – – – – – – – – –
                          _____
                          _____
                          – – – – – – – – – – – –

Name _____

Story Elements—Plot

Directions: The events in a story are part of the plot. Match each sequence word with the correct event from the story.

First

Big Thunder reads his son's heart.

Next

Thunder Boy Jr. is given his own name.

Lastly

Thunder Boy Jr. says he doesn't want to be small.

Vocabulary Overview

Key words and phrases from this section are provided below with definitions and sentences about how the words are used in the story. Introduce and discuss these important vocabulary words with students. If you think these words or other words in the story warrant more time devoted to them, there are suggestions in the introduction for other vocabulary activities (page 5).

Word or Phrase	Definition	Sentence about Text
Jr.	junior; a son with the same name as his father	People call him Thunder Boy **Jr.** because he is named after his father, Thunder Boy.
storm	an extreme type of weather	Thunder is a **storm** that fills up the sky.
fancy	not plain	Agnes and Lillian are **fancy** names.
mountain	big piece of land that is taller than a hill	Thunder Boy Jr. says he once climbed a **mountain**.
mud	mixture of water and dirt	Thunder Boy Jr. thinks **Mud in His Ears** would be a good name.
grass dancer	someone who performs a style of powwow dancing	Thunder Boy Jr. is a **grass dancer**.
traveling	going on a journey	Thunder Boy Jr. dreams of **traveling** the world.

Name _____

Vocabulary Activity

Directions: Choose four words from the story. Draw pictures that show what these words mean. Label the pictures.

_____   _____

- - - - - - - - - - - - - - -   - - - - - - - - - - - - - - -

_____   _____

_____   _____

- - - - - - - - - - - - - - -   - - - - - - - - - - - - - - -

_____   _____

Analyzing the Literature

Provided below are discussion questions you can use in small groups, with the whole class, or for written assignments. Each question is written at two levels so that you can choose the right question for each group of students. For each question, a few key points are provided for your reference as you discuss the book with students.

Story Element	Level 1	Level 2	Key Discussion Points
Plot	Look closely at the pictures on the pages about the orca and the mountain. What do you notice?	Thunder Boy Jr. says he has touched an orca and climbed a mountain. What do the illustrations tell you?	The illustrations show that Thunder Boy Jr. is imaginative. The orca is actually Big Thunder wearing a mask. The mountain that Thunder Boy Jr. climbs is actually Big Thunder covered in a blanket. This suggests that Big Thunder is a big, towering man.
Setting	What are some of the animals you see in the book?	Why might the illustrator choose to show certain animals in the book?	The animals shown are an orca, a coyote, a bear, and a snake. The illustrator probably chooses these animals because they are important in American Indian culture.
Character	How does Thunder Boy Jr. come up with new names for himself?	What might the events in Thunder Boy Jr.'s life have to do with his search for a new name?	Thunder Boy Jr. uses his favorite activities and things he has done to come up with new names. He is searching for a name that captures his experiences and reflects his feelings about himself as a brave, adventurous, independent person.
Plot	Look at the illustration on the page with "I hate my name!" in big letters. What is happening?	What are the coyote, snake, and bear doing when Thunder Boy Jr. says he hates his name?	The animals seem to be yelling, "I hate my name" along with Thunder Boy Jr. This helps to express his feeling more powerfully. There are also two bolts of lightning, which act as foreshadowing.

Name _____

Reader Response

Think

Thunder Boy Jr. wants a new name. He tries to come up with one on his own. Then, his dad finally gives him one—Lightning!

Opinion Writing Prompt

Do you think Lightning is a good name for Thunder Boy Jr.? Why or why not? If you can think of a better name, tell what it is and what makes it better.

_____

_____

_____

_____

_____

_____

_____

_____

_____

_____

_____

_____

Guided close Reading

Closely reread the pages where we first meet Thunder Boy Jr. Start at the beginning. Stop with, "Thunder Boy Smith Jr." Pay close attention to the pictures.

Directions: Think about these questions. In the space below, write ideas or draw pictures as you think. Be ready to share your answers.

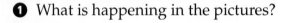

❶ What is happening in the pictures?

❷ What do you know about the relationship between Thunder Boy Jr. and his sister?

❸ Why do Thunder Boy Jr.'s parents look disappointed?

Name _____

Making connections— Honoring Heritage

Directions: Thunder Boy Jr. is an American Indian. He honors his heritage by powwow dancing. Write about what you do to honor your heritage. Then, draw a picture to go with it. Model your drawing after the ones in the book.

_____

_ _ _ _ _ _ _ _ _ _ _ _ _ _ _ _ _ _ _

_____

_ _ _ _ _ _ _ _ _ _ _ _ _ _ _ _ _ _ _

_____

_ _ _ _ _ _ _ _ _ _ _ _ _ _ _ _ _ _ _

_____

_ _ _ _ _ _ _ _ _ _ _ _ _ _ _ _ _ _ _

_____

Language Learning—Antonyms

Directions: Look at the list of words from the book. Write a word that means the opposite of each. Then, write a sentence using each antonym.

Language Hint!

Antonyms are words that have opposite meanings.

Word	Antonym	Sentence
normal	unusual	Thunder Boy is an unusual name.
real		
good		
big		
close		
whisper		
hate		
wrong		

Name _____

Story Elements—Plot

Directions: A red ball appears on ten different pages in the book. Follow the ball. Make a list of who has the ball on each page.

1. _____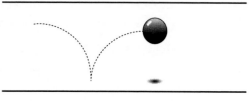

6. _____

2. _____

7. _____

3. _____

8. _____

4. _____

9. _____

5. _____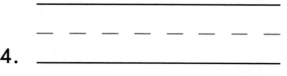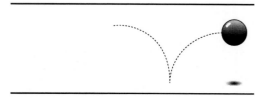

10. _____

Name _____

Story Elements—Setting

Directions: Imagine *Thunder Boy Jr.* was set in a city. Find the pictures in the book that match the names below. What changes you would make to these pictures? Draw the new pictures.

Touch the Clouds

Full of Wonder

Vocabulary Overview

Key words from this section are provided below with definitions and sentences about how the words are used in the story. Introduce and discuss these important vocabulary words with students. If you think these words or other words in the story warrant more time devoted to them, there are suggestions in the introduction for other vocabulary activities (page 5).

Word	Definition	Sentence about Text
birth	when someone is born	Thunder Boy gets his name at **birth**.
hate	extreme dislike	Thunder Boy Jr. **hates** his name.
cool	excellent	Thunder Boy Jr. wants a name that describes something **cool** that he's done.
thousand	the number 1,000	A name that might fit is Not Afraid of Ten **Thousand** Teeth.
chase	quickly follow	Thunder Boy Jr.'s dog likes to **chase** his tail.
lightning	flash or bolt of light from the clouds	Thunder Boy Jr. is now known as **Lightning**.
amazing	wonderful	Lightning and his dad will create **amazing** weather together.

Vocabulary Activity

Directions: Use a word from the story to complete each sentence.

Words from the Story

amazing	birth	chase	cool	Lightning

1. Thunder Boy Jr. was given his name at _____.

2. Thunder Boy Jr. wants a _____ name.

3. They will make _____ weather.

4. Thunder Boy Jr.'s new name is _____.

5. The dog likes to _____ his tail.

Teacher Plans

Analyzing the Literature

Provided below are discussion questions you can use in small groups, with the whole class, or for written assignments. Each question is written at two levels so that you can choose the right question for each group of students. For each question, a few key points are provided for your reference as you discuss the book with students.

Story Element	Level 1	Level 2	Key Discussion Points
Character	Look at the page that says "Big Thunder" in large letters. What is the difference in the way "Little Thunder" is written?	Look at the page that says "Big Thunder" in large letters. What does the difference in letter size tell you about the characters?	"Big Thunder" is set in large type, while "Little Thunder" is set in much smaller type. This is a visual way of conveying how Thunder Boy Jr. feels about his nickname. He is smaller than and might feel overshadowed by his father.
Setting	Look at the page that says "Lightning!" in big letters. What is happening with the weather?	How does the weather show how Lightning (Thunder Boy Jr.) feels about his new name? How can you tell?	The weather is rainy and cloudy, and there are lightning bolts. The lightning bolts look as though they are coming from Lightning. It makes him look happy and powerful. Big Thunder is carrying Lightning away from the rain, which shows that he is protecting Lightning from his old sadness of not having his own name.
Plot	Some of the words are inside speech bubbles. What does this mean? Find at least one example.	Why do you think the narrator tells some of the story in speech bubbles?	Speech bubbles show words coming directly from a character's mouth. The narrator tells some of the story in speech bubbles to show that some of the characters are talking to or calling for Thunder Boy Jr.
Setting	What is the setting on the first page? What is the setting on the last page?	What changes in the setting? What does this tell you about how the characters change?	The book begins with Thunder Boy Jr. standing on a chair trying to play his father's guitar. It ends with him sitting on his father's shoulders. This shows that father and son have grown together. It may also indicate that Thunder Boy Jr. doesn't feel the need to act out any longer now that he has his own unique identity.

Reader Response

Think

Thunder Boy Jr. tells the reader about some of the things he has done. He also tells about what he wants to do.

Narrative Writing Prompt

Write a story that tells the next chapter in Thunder Boy Jr.'s life. What do you think he'll do now that he has his own name?

_____

- -

_____

_____

- -

_____

_____

- -

_____

_____

- -

_____

_____

- -

_____

Name _____

Guided close Reading

Closely reread
the pages where
Thunder Boy Jr.
gets his new name.

Directions: Think about
these questions. In
the space below, write
ideas or draw pictures
as you think. Be ready
to share your answers.

❶ What is Thunder Boy Jr.'s new name? Why is it written in such big letters?

❷ How does Thunder Boy Jr. feel about his new name? How can you tell?

❸ How do the other characters feel about the name?

Making connections—Grass Dancing

Directions: Thunder Boy Jr. is a grass dancer. The grass dance is an American Indian art form. Grass dancers wear special outfits. Find pictures of grass dancing in books or on the Internet. Draw your own picture of a grass dance.

Language Learning—Synonyms

Directions: Write synonyms for the words from *Thunder Boy Jr.*

Language Hint!

Synonyms are words that have almost the same meaning.

Word	Synonym
awesome	
cool	
little	
exactly	
amazing	

Story Elements—Setting

Directions: Look at the page that says "Big Thunder."
Look at the page that says "Lightning!" The pages are
similar to each other. They are also different. Use the
Venn diagram to compare and contrast the pages.

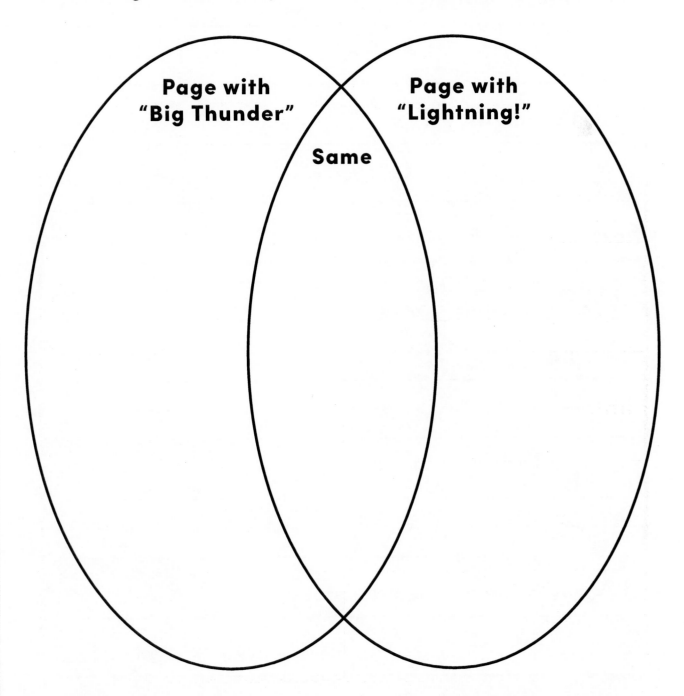

Page with
"Big Thunder"

Same

Page with
"Lightning!"

Name _____

Story Elements—Plot

Directions: Summarize the plot of *Thunder Boy Jr.* Your summary should tell what happens in order. It should also tell the problem and the solution.

The problem is that

_____

- - - - - - - - - - - - - - - - - - -

_____.

First, Thunder Boy Jr.

_____

- - - - - - - - - - - - - - - - - - -

_____.

Next, he

_____

- - - - - - - - - - - - - - - - - - -

_____.

Then, he

_____

- - - - - - - - - - - - - - - - - - -

_____.

Finally,

_____

- - - - - - - - - - - - - - - - - - -

_____.

This solves the problem because

_____

- - - - - - - - - - - - - - - - - - -

_____.

Name _____

Post-Reading Theme Thoughts

Directions: Choose a main character from *Thunder Boy Jr.* Pretend you are that character. Draw a picture of a happy face or a sad face to show how the character would feel about each statement. Then, use words to explain your picture.

Character I Chose: _____

Statement	How Do You Feel? ☺ ☹	Explain Your Answer
Names are important.		
I like my name.		
I want a different name.		
I have many name ideas.		

Culminating Activity: Choosing a Nickname

Directions: Thunder Boy Jr. wants a new name. Throughout the book, he tries to find new names. He explores his accomplishments (climbing a mountain, touching an orca), his favorite activities (garage sales, dancing), and his dreams (traveling the world). Give students the opportunity to do the same. Through a self-portrait, an interview with someone who knows them, and a brief writing assignment, students will choose new nicknames for themselves.

Self-Portrait—Draw students' attention to the style the illustrator uses throughout the book. Discuss the energy in the pictures where Thunder Boy Jr. is thinking of new names. On page 61, have students draw self-portraits. Each student's picture should show the student engaged in an activity that makes him or her feel proud. Students can use any medium you provide them, but cutting the figures from construction paper will help students mimic the book's style.

Interview—Have students identify a person they can interview who knows them well, such as a family member or a close friend. Discuss the types of interview questions that will help them learn about themselves. As a class, create a list of possible questions individuals can draw upon if they need more ideas. For example, "What are three words you would use to describe me?" Provide students time to conduct their interviews either during the school day or as part of a homework assignment. Have students record the questions and answers on page 62.

My Nickname—Using the form on page 63, students combine the information from their self-portraits and the interviews to create nicknames for themselves. Students explain how they arrived at the names and why they are good choices.

culminating Activity:
choosing a Nickname (cont.)

Self-Portrait

Directions: A self-portrait is a picture of you. Show yourself doing something that makes you feel proud. Create the picture in the same style as the illustrations in *Thunder Boy Jr.*

Name _____

Culminating Activity: Choosing a Nickname (cont.)

Interview

Directions: Think about a person who knows you well. Write two questions you would like to ask the person. Then, interview the person and write the answers below.

_____

Question 1: _____

_____

Answer: _____

_____

Question 2: _____

_____

Answer: _____

_____

culminating Activity:
choosing a Nickname (cont.)

My Nickname

Directions: Think about your self-portrait. What does it tell about you? Think about the interview. What did you learn about yourself? Use this information to choose a nickname for yourself. Explain how you decided on the nickname. What makes it a good one for you?

_____

– – – – – – – – – – – – – – – – –

My Nickname _____

How I Chose It and Why It's a Good Nickname

_____

– – – – – – – – – – – – – – – – –

_____

_____

– – – – – – – – – – – – – – – – –

_____

_____

– – – – – – – – – – – – – – – – –

_____

_____

– – – – – – – – – – – – – – – – –

_____

Name _____

comprehension Assessment

Directions: Fill in the bubble for the best response to each question.

Section 1—Meet Thunder Boy Jr.

1. What best describes the name Thunder Boy?

(A) There is only one Thunder Boy.

(B) It is a normal name.

(C) Thunder Boy Jr. is named after his father.

(D) Thunder Boy Jr. plays the guitar.

Section 2—I Want a New Name

2. How does Thunder Boy Jr. get ideas for new names?

(A) He asks his parents for ideas.

(B) He gets ideas from things he has done.

(C) He travels the world looking for names.

(D) He gets mud in his ears.

Section 3—Thunder Boy and Lightning

3. Which is **not** a reason that Lightning says, "Together, my dad and I will become amazing weather"?

(A) Lightning loves his new name.

(B) Thunder and lightning go together.

(C) He is tired of storms.

(D) Thunder and Lightning will light up the sky.

comprehension Assessment (cont.)

Section 4—Illustrations

4. Why does the illustrator show Thunder Boy Jr.'s family throughout the book?

_____

- -

_____

_____

- -

_____

_____

- -

_____

_____

- -

_____

Section 5—Whole Book

5. What does Thunder Boy Jr. mean when he says, "I don't want to be small"?

(A) He doesn't want to be a small copy of his dad.

(B) He wants to grow up to be like his dad.

(C) He wishes he was just as tall as his dad.

(D) He wants to stay little.

Response to Literature: My Favorite Illustration

Directions: *Thunder Boy Jr.* is full of cool illustrations. Look through the book and choose the illustration you like the best. Draw your own version of the illustration in the frame. Then, answer the questions on the next page.

Response to Literature:
My Favorite Illustration

Directions: Think about the illustration you drew on page 66, and answer the questions.

1. Describe the scene in your illustration. Who is in it?
   What is happening?

   _____

   _____

   _____

   _____

   _____

2. Why is this your favorite illustration in the book?

   _____

   _____

   _____

   _____

   _____

3. What is something that you would like to tell the
   illustrator of *Thunder Boy Jr.?*

   _____

   _____

   _____

   _____

   _____

Name _____

Response to Literature Rubric

Directions: Use this rubric to evaluate student responses.

Great Job	Good Work	Keep Trying
☐ You answered all three questions completely. You included many details.	☐ You answered all three questions.	☐ You did not answer all three questions.
☐ Your handwriting is very neat. There are no spelling errors.	☐ Your handwriting can be neater. There are some spelling errors.	☐ Your handwriting is not very neat. There are many spelling errors.
☐ Your picture is neat and fully colored.	☐ Your picture is neat, and some of it is colored.	☐ Your picture is not very neat and/or fully colored.
☐ Creativity is clear in the picture and the writing.	☐ Creativity is clear in either the picture or the writing.	☐ There is not much creativity in either the picture or the writing.

Teacher Comments: _____

_____

_____

_____

Name _____

_____

- - - - - - - - - - - - - - - - - -

_____

_____

- - - - - - - - - - - - - - - - - -

_____

_____

- - - - - - - - - - - - - - - - - -

_____

_____

- - - - - - - - - - - - - - - - - -

_____

The responses provided here are just examples of what the students may answer. Many accurate responses are possible for the questions throughout this unit.

Vocabulary Activity—Section 1:
Meet Thunder Boy Jr. (page 15)

1. awesome
2. real
3. secret
4. thunder
5. whisper

Guided Close Reading—Section 1:
Meet Thunder Boy Jr. (page 18)

1. Thunder Boy Jr. is on a chair "playing" a guitar. The strings break. Then, he gets in trouble for breaking the strings.
2. The family seems close. Lillian seems to adore her older brother, even though he teases her. The parents seem caring.
3. Thunder Boy Jr. likes the name Sam. You can tell because he says it is a "good" and "normal" name.

Language Learning—Section 1:
Meet Thunder Boy Jr. (page 20)

1. People **call** him Big Thunder.
2. His dad **gave** his name to him at birth.
3. A storm **fills** the sky.
4. Thunder Boy Jr. **tells** a secret.
5. He **whispers** the secret.
6. Thunder Boy Jr. **calls** his dad awesome.

Story Elements—Section 2:
Meet Thunder Boy Jr. (page 22)

- Readers learn Thunder Boy Jr. is his real name.
- Thunder Boy Jr. tells the reader that his name is not normal.
- Readers learn that Thunder Boy Jr. is named after his dad.
- Thunder Boy Jr. tells the names of his mother and sister.
- Thunder Boy Jr. tells the reader a secret.
- Readers learn how Thunder Boy Jr. feels about his dad.

Vocabulary Activity—Section 2:
I Want a New Name (page 24)

1. Thunder Boy Jr. is full of **wonder** because he wants to travel the world.

Guided Close Reading—Section 2
I Want a New Name (page 27)

1. The names Thunder Boy Jr. thinks of include: Not Afraid of Ten Thousand Teeth; Touch the Clouds; Mud in His Ears; Gravity's Best Friend; Star Boy; Old Toys Are Awesome; Can't Run Fast While Laughing; Drums, Drums, and More Drums; Full of Wonder. Student choices for favorite name will vary.
2. He goes with his mom. They might ride on her motorcycle since the picture shows it.
3. The drummers are the bear, the coyote, and the snake. They also appear when Thunder Boy Jr. screams that he hates his name.

Language Learning—Section 2
I Want a New Name (page 29)

Students' lists of nouns will vary but might include: *alligator, robot, toy, horse, dog, doll, rattle, elephant, top.*

Story Elements—Section 2
I Want a New Name (page 30)

- He touches an orca.—brave/adventurous
- He climbs a mountain.—adventurous/brave
- He slides through mud.—playful
- He rides a bike when he is three years old.—athletic

Guided Close Reading—Section 3
Thunder Boy and Lightning (page 36)

1. His dad says "Little Thunder" and reaches out toward him. It is obvious it's his dad because the next page shows his dad holding him up.

2. Thunder Boy Jr. looks upset. He is not smiling. He is sitting with his legs curled up to his chest.

3. Thunder Boy Jr. says he loves his dad to make sure the reader knows that wanting his own name doesn't mean he does not care about his dad.

Language Learning—Section 3
Thunder Boy and Lightning (page 38)

Adjective	Noun	Adjective + Noun
little	Thunder	Little Thunder
amazing	weather	amazing weather
bright	love	bright love
loud	love	loud love

Story Elements—Section 3
Thunder Boy and Lightning (page 40)

- First—Thunder Boy Jr. says he doesn't want to be small.
- Next—Big Thunder reads his son's heart.
- Lastly—Thunder Boy Jr. is given his own name.

Guided Close Reading—Section 4
Illustrations (page 45)

1. Thunder Boy Jr. is playing with a guitar. His sister is playing with a red ball. When Thunder Boy Jr. gets in trouble for breaking the guitar strings, he takes the ball from his sister.

2. You can tell that Thunder Boy Jr. is older than his sister. He is bigger than her. It looks as though she might follow him around the way younger siblings often do.

3. Thunder Boy Jr.'s parents look disappointed because he has taken the ball from his sister and has made her cry.

Language Learning—Section 4
Illustrations (page 47)

Word	Antonym
normal	unusual
real	fake
good	bad
big	little
close	far
whisper	yell
hate	love
wrong	right

Story Elements—Section 4
Illustrations (page 48)

1. sister/Lillian
2. sister/Lillian
3. Thunder Boy Jr.
4. Thunder Boy Jr.
5. Thunder Boy Jr. and sister/Lillian
6. sister/Lillian
7. dad/Big Thunder
8. sister/Lillian
9. sister/Lillian
10. Thunder Boy Jr.

Vocabulary Activity—Section 5
Whole Book (page 51)

1. birth
2. cool
3. amazing
4. Lightning
5. chase

Guided Close Reading—Section 5
Whole Book (page 54)

1. Thunder Boy Jr.'s new name is Lightning. It is written in big letters to show that Lightning is excited about and likes his new name.

2. Thunder Boy Jr. is happy about his new name. You can tell because he is smiling and talks about lighting up the sky with his dad.

3. Everyone likes Thunder Boy Jr.'s new name. You can tell because his sister looks happy, and his dad is smiling.

Language Learning—Section 5
Whole Book (page 56)

Word	Synonym
awesome	outstanding; cool
cool	terrific; awesome
little	small
exactly	same; equal
amazing	wonderful

Story Elements—Section 5
Whole Book (page 57)

Page with "Big Thunder"
- Dad looks angry.
- Thunder Boy Jr. and his sister are fighting over the red ball.

Page with "Lightning"
- Dad looks happy.
- Thunder Boy Jr. has the ball.
- His sister looks happy.
- The dog is shown on the page.

Same
- Gray clouds
- lightning strikes
- Both show Dad, Thunder Boy Jr. and his sister

Story Elements—Section 5
Whole Book (page 58)

The problem is that Thunder Boy Jr. hates his name.

First, Thunder Boy Jr. tells why he hates his name.

Next, he tries to come up with different names.

Then, he says he wants to be himself.

Finally, his dad gives him a new name.

This solves the problem because Thunder Boy Jr. loves his new name.

Comprehension Assessment (pages 64–65)

1. C. Thunder Boy Jr. is named after his father.

2. B. He gets ideas from things he has done.

3. C. He is tired of storms.

4. The illustrator shows Thunder Boy Jr.'s family to show the reader that his family is important to him and plays a big role in his life and who he is.

5. A. He doesn't want to be a small copy of his dad.